An Introvert's Guide
to Being Social

By

Stefan Cain

This page intentionally left blank.

About the Author

Stefan Cain is a dog lover, father of three, and a therapist, specializing in social skills and anxiety. As an introvert himself, he knows firsthand the types of struggles and issues that sociability can cause. He grew up as the shy, quiet kid with very few friends (a constant source of worry for his mother) and that trend, he says, probably would have continued through college and perhaps his entire life, if he had not met his future wife, Katie, who was a psychology major at the university he attended. It was she who first taught him about personality types, coping skills, and many of the other topics covered in this book. The result? He switched majors, proposed to Katie, and, eventually, started his own practice aimed at helping others deal with the same struggles he once faced.

Stefan Cain has spent the majority of his working career in numerous academic research positions, working on a wealth of psychological, societal and cultural topics. His research work and adept studies have been used to form the backbone of many popular titles available today, providing him with the experience and hunger to delve deeper into some avenues of thought.

Alongside his serious academic work, Stefan has been published in a number of prominent publications; filing news reports, features and insightful opinion pieces on myriad topics throughout his career.

About this Book

Introvert's Guide to Being Social, written by Stefan Cain who's a self-professed introvert is an easy-to-read, practical guide on how introverts can learn to better understand themselves and improve their communication and networking skills. Beginning with an analysis of what it actually means to be an introvert or extrovert (from a scientific, psychological perspective), Stefan Cain explains what makes someone an introvert or extrovert and how that particular trait manifests itself in everyday life. The second half of the book is devoted to laying out a game plan for introverts in regards to social situations, focusing particularly on those that occur within the workplace or professional sphere. Inside Introvert's Guide to Being Social, you'll learn how to prepare yourself for social situations, as well as tips, tricks, strategies, exercises, and information on effective communication. If you've ever found yourself frozen in conversation, sweating nervously at a party, dreading office events, and making up bizarre excuses in order to get out of social occasions, then this book is for you.

This page intentionally left blank.

CONTENTS

INTRODUCTION

When I was first trying to think up titles for this book, one of the ones suggested was something like "How to Become the Popular Introvert." That, in one phrase, sums up a misconception about introverts—that they want popularity but just do not know how to attain it. I would argue that introverts prefer to be alone, in a small group, or one-on-one, but they recognize the benefits that come with popularity, such as better networking, better chances at attracting a partner, better job prospects, etc. In this sense, popularity, being well-received by others, is only a tool, a means to an end. That is how I approached this topic. As an introvert myself, I realized that my lack of extrovert traits (technically, the spelling is "extravert" but since "extrovert" is more commonly used in general discussion, that is what I will be using) tendencies were holding me back from accomplishing my goals and keeping me from the things I wanted. So I had to make a choice—did I want to learn how to use extrovert traits to achieve what I wanted, or did I want to keep letting the world's preference for extroversion drag me down. In the end, I chose the former, and I'm glad that I did.

This book is for the people who need real strategies and solutions to surviving and thriving in a world that values extroversion much more highly than it does introversion (more on that in Chapter 3). It's about accepting reality and learning how to play by its rules. If you want to stage an introvert revolution, refuse to move outside of your introverted-ness, and try to make the world appreciate introverts, that's fine. But if your goal is to find success in your own life, then this is your book. Here's what you'll be learning:

Chapter 1: Introverts: Fiction and Fact

This is just a simple little intro that addresses the misconceptions about introversion and extroversion, as those terms have become somewhat muddied since being adopted by the general public.

Chapter 2: The Psychology of Introversion and Extroversion

Here we talk about the science behind the "introvert" and "extrovert" labels, discussing the theories that support it, its physiological component, and how all of that shows itself through a person's actions.

Chapter 3: Introverts in an Extroverted World

This chapter discusses the way the Western world values certain personality traits over others and the effects that those preferences have on an individual, as well as a societal, level.

Chapter 4: Attitude and Approach

This is where we start getting into the meat of the book. This chapter is about reflecting on both how you think and on your natural reactions to certain situations, how that applies to the introversion-extroversion trait, and how to train your brain to make certain situations more bearable or maybe even pleasant.

Chapter 5: Social Preparation

This chapter discusses different actions you can take before having to engage in social activity in order to make yourself feel more comfortable and at-ease and, hopefully, have more success.

Chapter 6: The Importance of Good Communication Skills

This is an introductory chapter on communication skills that talks about their importance, the ways in which we communicate, qualities of a good communicator, and the differences in the ways that introverts and extroverts communicate.

Chapter 7: Improving Your Verbal Communication

Chapter 7 goes in-depth about verbal communication skills and what it entails. The majority of the chapter will talk about the different techniques and skills that you can use to become a more effective verbal communicator, as well as a rather lengthy discussion on the importance of small talk.

Chapter 8: Nonverbal Communication

This discusses the importance that nonverbal cues play in our interactions with others, as well as how to better identify what other people are saying with their body language while ensuring that you know how to use your body to make nonverbal statements.

Chapter 9: Introverts in the Workplace

Chapter nine briefly covers some of the issues that most often arise for introverts when they are at work.

INTROVERTS: FICTION AND FACT

When it comes to introversion and extroversion, there is a lot of false information out there. It's typically spread by people who sort of know what they are talking about, but not really. That's why this section is here—to clear up some of that mess.

Misconception #1: Introverts are shy.

Introversion and shyness are often equated in popular literature and in the media, but they are not the same thing. Both are related to socializing, but shyness is actually a form of anxiety, where an individual fears rejection, embarrassment, or ridicule, causing them to actively avoid social activities even if they do actually want to participate. Introverts, however, do not fear social interaction; they simply do not have much of an interest in it. (More on that in the next chapter) Now, there can be shy introverts—they do exist—but introverts are not automatically shy and all shy people are not automatically introverts. Yes, extroverts can be shy as well.

Misconception #2: Introverts are unsocial/Introverts hate people

As an introvert myself, this is one of the more irritating misconceptions—the idea that I and my fellow introverts are misanthropic, grouchy hermits who would rather eat lunch with ravenous sharks than interact with other humans. While this may be true in some cases, it is certainly not the rule. Introverts have different social needs than their extroverted counterparts and this means that they tend to socialize differently. You are not likely to find an introvert entertaining a large group of acquaintances with an amusing anecdote, but rather on the outskirts of the group, observing and listening, or off somewhere in a one-on-one conversation that has actual depth. With introverts, the phrase "quality over quantity" accurately sums up how most feel about relationships; introverts tend to have fewer friends, but they have deeper, closer connections to them.

Misconception #3: Introverts are sad/lonely/depressed

Extroverts tend to think that introverts are sad and depressed because the latter likes to spend so much time alone. For an extrovert, being alone for too long makes them sad, because they get their energy from social interaction and prefer to be around people. It is hard for them to understand that a person might actually *enjoy* being alone, as is the case with most introverts. In other words, they project how they feel onto us; they assume that because they are depressed when left alone for too long, that we must also be the same way, which could explain why so many well-meaning extroverts try to "fix" their introverted friends and family.

Misconception #4: Introverts are inherently more creative/intelligent/sensitive/intellectual than extroverts.

While it is true that many great thinkers, such as Bill Gates or Albert Einstein, have been introverts, that does not necessarily mean that introverts automatically have an intellectual advantage over extroverts. Extroverts can be just as smart, innovative, and creative as introverts. Introverts are often thought of as being "deeper" than extroverts (and many introverts think this about themselves as well) because we tend to be more introspective, but this is not true either. Extroverts can be deep thinkers as well.

Misconception #4: You're either an introvert or an extrovert.

Everybody has both introverted and extroverted traits within them. What makes a person one or the other is a matter of which trait set is dominant. It is helpful to think of personality as a continuum, with introversion and extroversion at opposite ends of the spectrum. A person may land anywhere between the two, but in most cases, an individual will fall closer to one end than the other. However, every individual has traits of both. (It has been suggested that there is a third type, the ambivert, that exists in the middle of the two, but that is a discussion outside of the scope of this book).

Misconception #5: Introverts are failed extroverts/Introverts want to be extroverts

Western society tends to value the traits of extroverts (charismatic, personable, gregarious, etc.) over those of introverts, which has led to introversion being the "undesirable" or "incomplete" personality type. Now, some introverts may want to be extroverts simply because the world is more accepting of the latter, but that is not automatically the case. Introverts think and act *differently*, not automatically incorrectly. (More on this in Chapter 3)

Misconception #6: Introverts can become extroverts if they really want to do so.

Nope. Sorry to burst any bubbles, but introversion and extroversion are inborn personality types that cannot be changed permanently. Now, introverts may draw upon their extrovert traits to act like extroverts in certain situations, but that does not change anything on a psychological or biological level. What introverts should realize is that not only can they draw upon their more extroverted traits to be more successful, they can also use their introvert strengths to do so as well—and that is what this book is all about.

THE PSYCHOLOGY OF INTROVERSION AND EXTROVERSION

In Chapter 1, we talked about some of the incorrect ideas that people have about introverts and to some extent, extroverts. Now it's time to paint a lovely and cohesive picture of what it *actually* means to be either introverted or extroverted, going back to the original definitions and theories established by psychologists, rather than relying on the bastardized versions used today.

THE SCIENCE OF PERSONALITY

What is personality? Ask this question to 100 different scientists or researchers who specialize in its study and you will receive 100 different answers. How do we measure it? How do we study and classify it? Where does it come from and what influences it? There are a number of different methods that scientists have used to study it, but there are no solid answers to these questions. The field is full of theories, proposed definitions, and theoretical models. However, all of this uncertainty proves one undeniable truth—that the concept of personality is a complex one that, on an academic level, is not yet understood enough for those working in the field to reach any kind of consensus, and that on an individual level, is comprised of any number of variables, some of which defy classification.

I say all of this to emphasize that, while introversion/extroversion is one of the more well-known dimensions of personality, it still only makes up one aspect of who you are as a person. You may have heard of something called the "Big Five" or "the five factor model"—this is currently one of the more popular theories used to describe personality. It divides the human personality into five broad traits: extroversion, neuroticism, agreeableness, openness, and conscientiousness. Notice that one's level of extroversion is only one of the five dimensions. Those other four affect you as well. While this book seeks to help you address and overcome some of those challenges associated with introversion, it is outside of the scope of this book to include discussions of the other four dimensions. However, you would be best served by thinking about your other defining qualities as you read, so that you can integrate them into your approach.

INTROVERSION-EXTROVERSION: BIOLOGICALLY BASED

The concepts of introversion and extroversion form the basis of one of the most famous type-trait theories of personality, which was developed by Carl Jung, a Swiss psychiatrist working in the early twentieth century. Jung identified two fundamental orientations or attitudes which have a wide range of manifestations; an individual's orientation is innate and biologically based (thus why introverts cannot "become" extroverts) and determines whether they are oriented towards the outside world—the extraverts (yes, with an "a", though now "extrovert" with an "o" is used more frequently, thus why I have decided to use it for this book, as it is what the general population is most used to seeing.)—or if their focus is more inward—the introverts. People have traits of both, but, according to Jung, each person favors one side more heavily than the other. This is why you, an introvert, sometimes crave human interaction, or feel an unusually strong desire to go to a party, and why an extrovert may sometimes feel as if they would rather do something besides socializing.

In the 1960s, Hans Eysenck further theorized about the neurobiological basis for the introversion-extroversion trait, offering at least a partial answer as to why extroverts and introverts react differently to the same situations. He postulated that extroverts have a lower basic rate of arousal than their introverted counterparts. *Arousal*, in this context, refers to the extent to which the mind and body are ready to respond to stimulation. If Eysenck's theory were true, it would mean that extroverted individuals require more stimulation in order to feel pleasure, or at least normal. Introverts, conversely, would have normal basic arousal rates or higher basic arousal rates; this means that they do not require extra stimulation.

Eysenck's theory fits well with the tendency of introverts to feel overstimulated in the same environments that energize extroverts.

Thankfully, technology and scientific innovation have improved drastically since Eysenck and Jung's days, meaning that we now have viable means to test various psychological theories in such a way as to prove or disprove the existence of a physiological component to psychological events, as well as a way to refine earlier theories to fit with physical evidence. Simply stated, this means "we have brain scans now." And because we now have these capabilities, we have been able to physically test what was previously untestable.

Faces and Flowers

Researcher Inna Fishman of the Salk Institute for Biological Sciences and her colleagues designed a test that would measure the electrical activity (known as P300) of the brains of individuals that were tested as introverted, mildly extroverted, and very extroverted in response to social situations. A change in a brain's P300, which shows up on an EEG, can be caused by an alteration in the environment. This change occurs within 300 milliseconds, well before the person is even aware of it. For this test, subjects were shown a set of images—a series of male faces interspersed with female faces mixed with a series of purple flowers interspersed with yellow flowers. The idea was that, if Jung and Eysenck's theories held true, extroverts would show greater response to the social stimuli—the pictures of the human faces. And that is exactly what happened. Those participants who scored higher on the test for extroversion showed greater P300 responses to the human faces than those who scored lower. Introverts, however, showed similar responses to both the flowers and the faces.

This means that extroverts paid greater attention to social stimuli than they did non-social stimuli, while the brains of introverts made very little distinction between the two. These results show that introverts deal with their interactions with people in pretty much the same way as they do with all other external, non-human stimuli.

The Pleasure of Rewards

A study conducted in the early 2000s measured how the brains of introverts and extroverts reacted to rewards. Participants filled out a personality profile and gave researchers a genetic sample in the form of a mouth swab. They were then hooked up to a brain scanner and asked to do a gambling task. Scientists then analyzed the results, comparing the brain scans of introverts to those of the extroverted volunteers. The brains of the extroverts showed a greater response than those of introverts when the gambles they took paid off. The activity was most noticeable in the extroverts' amygdala, which processes emotional stimuli, and the nucleus accumbens, which is a part of the brain's reward circuitry and dopamine system. Additionally, when researchers analyzed the results of the genetic testing, those individuals who showed more response in reaction to a successful gamble (the extroverts) were also shown to have a gene that increases the responsiveness of the brain to dopamine.

Dopamine is a neurotransmitter that affects our emotional reactions, such as our levels of excitement. It's the chemical that causes that "buzz" feeling after something good happens. When dopamine releases into the brain, we become more talkative, more willing to explore and take risks, and pay more attention to our surroundings.

Therefore, an extrovert's lower arousal rate and greater sensitivity to dopamine means that not only do they require more stimulation, but they are more affected by one of the neurotransmitters that cause excitement and feelings of elation. Introverts, on the other hand are not as susceptible to dopamine's effects, which is why they often seem more subdued and seem less driven.

WHAT IT MEANS TO BE INTROVERTED OR EXTROVERTED

So we have this trait that is biologically based, with clear physiological differences between the two orientations, but what does that mean? For too long, the modern interpretation of the word "introvert" has been "someone who doesn't like people," but not only is this not true, it is a very shallow, one-dimensional definition that fails to fully evaluate the effects of having a certain orientation, as well as failing to highlight the nuances inherent in both types.

A Question of Energy

For Jung, both orientations could be broadly characterized by the way in which individuals of each type received and directed their energy. Introverts receive their energy from inside themselves by "interacting" with the ideas, thoughts, reactions, and memories in their own heads (thus why introverts have a reputation for being introspective and reflective). Their energy is drained by interpersonal interaction and must be recharged by spending time alone. Conversely, extroverts are energized by interacting with the outside world and other people. Being social and "in the middle of things" pumps them up and keeps them going, while being alone brings them down.

Characteristic Comparison

An introvert's inward orientation combined with type-specific neurological patterns and responses influence many aspects of their life, from the types of activities that they typically enjoy to the way in which they make decisions to how they learn. (And that's just listing a few)

Stimulation Needs

Extroverts' need for more stimulation drives them to seek out external sources that can provide it. They feed off of interaction with the outside world, which is why they like group events and are generally more gregarious than their introverted peers. For our part, we introverts do not require as much stimulation and are easily overwhelmed when there is too much going on around us. Introverts' fuel source is internal, not external.

Sociability

Sociability is perhaps the most obvious difference between introverts and extroverts. Extroverts need to be around people in order to feel "right". They need the hustle and bustle of conversation and activity in order to be happy, which is why they usually prefer to not be alone or in their own head. They need to interact with the world outside of themselves. Introverts, on the other hand, prefer one-on-one conversations, small groups, and just being alone. The external stimulation that gives extroverts so much pleasure can cause introverts to feel great anxiety. Many introverts find that verbal communication is not the method of communication that best suits them, often opting for written communication instead. For example, if they needed to relay information to a work colleague, they most likely would not seek out that individual in person and talk to them face-to-face. Given the option, they will often choose to send emails.

Activity preferences

Extroverts prefer activities that involve others and they often have a hard time understanding that an introvert's desire to be alone is not usually a sign that something is wrong. Being alone for too long would make an extrovert unhappy and they assume it's the same way for us. But as introverts, we need that time to ourselves; it is what gives us energy. This is why introverts favor activities that can be done solo—reading, drawing, working puzzles, or just sitting somewhere quiet and thinking. Introverts don't mind having just their brain for company, so it makes sense that they would be drawn to activities and careers that require just that—their brainpower and themselves. Because many are able to really focus on one task, they are particularly well-suited to projects that require a great deal of detail and precision. That brings us to our next characteristic: thinking.

Thinking

Introverts and extroverts process information differently. Extroverts tend to think out loud, which is why they often appear to be "quicker" than their introverted colleagues. In a brainstorming session, for example, an extrovert will throw out ideas as they come into his/her mind, even if they are not that good. When an extrovert is given information, they often skip over the details in favor of a big-picture approach. If you were to send them a long email full of the specifics of a certain project, they would probably just skim it. Introverts tend to keep their fragments of thoughts and ideas inside their head as they process it and analyze it. If you ask an introvert a question, they will usually mull it over in their heads before speaking. They also prefer deep thinking (thus their disdain for small talk), so a question that you ask them is likely to receive a detailed and thought-out answer. This trait is one reason why introverts are often deemed shy and seen as not talkative, or not contributory in discussions. That's not necessarily the case; they just need time to give the subject their full attention. And as for not being talkative…well, anyone who has ever gotten into a conversation with an introvert about a specific hobby or interest of theirs knows that introverts can talkative—you just have to hit the right subject.

Rewards

Because extroverts have a more intense positive reaction to rewards, such as food, sex, or increased social standing, they are more likely to seek out situations in which they might be awarded. They take more risks and are generally more excited and engaged in the world around them and they have a preference for immediate gratification. Introverts, conversely, do not experience this type of overwhelmingly positive reaction to rewards and thus do not have the same kind of motivation to seek them out. They tend to be less focused on immediate gratification, causing them to be more thoughtful about different situations and more cautious.

Easily distracted, but are rarely bored

Introverts are easily overstimulated, causing them to become distracted easily when there is a lot going on around them. However, in a quiet, peaceful environment, they have the ability to super-focus on a task or hobby for hours at a time.

INTROVERTS IN AN EXTROVERTED WORLD

Anecdote time:

When I was about 10, I overheard my mother talking to an acquaintance while she, my brother, and I were all at a birthday party. This person (let's call her "Cheryl") asked my mother to point out her children. She easily found my older brother, who was in the middle of large gathering of other laughing, talking, and playing children. "Wow, he's quite the extravert, isn't he?" remarked Cheryl with a smile. My 10 year old eyes could see the pride exuding from every pore in my mother's skin when she answered, "Yes, he's quite the social butterfly. I have such a hard time keeping track of all of his friends." Cheryl then asked Mom to point me out to her. It took her longer to find me—I was in a plastic chair in a corner by myself, happily reading a book I had brought. "Is he in trouble? Is something wrong?" inquired Cheryl. "He's being really quiet." My mother sighed, "He's very introverted. We have so much trouble getting him to socialize with other kids his age." Cheryl nodded sympathetically, "Well, maybe he'll grow out of it. I'm sure he'll come out of his shell eventually." They then went back to talking about other things and I quickly lost interest in eavesdropping because I was 10 and had an attention span like that of a hyperactive puppy who had just seen a squirrel. However, overhearing this exchange was the first time I started to think that something was wrong with me. Unfortunately, my experience is not the exception—so many introverts grow up trying to fit into the extrovert ideal, believing that their true nature is wrong.

THE DEVELOPMENT OF THE EXTROVERT IDEAL

In her book, *Quiet: The Power of Introverts in a World That Won't Stop Talking*, Susan Cain does a marvelous job at tracing the development of the rise of the extroverted personality and its subsequent supplanting of introversion as the preferred personality type.

According to Cain, as well as some cultural historians, before the twentieth century, the ideal individual was characterized by her seriousness, honor, and disciplined nature, with a focus more on what a person was like in public, rather than being concerned with public perception. During the 1920s, however, there was a shift in the American economy, moving from a largely rural, agriculturally-based system into the Industrial Age, which was centered in cities. People flocked to metropolitan areas, leaving their rural communities and social and familial ties behind, to become urbanites sharing a living space and workplace with strangers. No longer were one's coworkers individuals known since childhood, but anonymous faces and personalities. Before, influence had depended on family ties or civic ties, but in the emerging business world, what fueled one's career was their ability to successfully interact with strangers. Of particular importance was (and is) a good first impression. In fact, there is a notable and quite interesting shift in the self-help literature that was available; moving into the 1920s, the focus is on one's outer presentation. Note the differences within the following examples:

According to the author of an 1876 work entitled *Character*:

> Indeed, we can always better understand and appreciate a man's real character by the manner in which he conducts himself towards those who are the most nearly related to him, and by his transaction of the seemingly commonplace details of daily duty, than by his public exhibition of himself as an author, an orator, or a statesman. (*Character*, 3)

Here, the ideal qualities are said to be dutifulness, no matter what the task, and his treatment of and loyalty to those close to him in his inner or personal life. Contrast that with the advice given in the *Retail Salesmanship Source Book*, published in 1921:

> As the first impression comes first, it is of first importance. It is the gateway to success in selling…The control of yourself and the ability to radiate cordiality and good-will are things which must be cultivated and maintained…It is necessary for you to have yourself under such control that you can immediately bring the best of you into your face and manner,

that you may make a good first impression at the start. (*Retail Salesmanship Source Book*, 223-224)

Notice how much emphasis is put on one's appearance and body language and, by extension, one's ability to manipulate the latter. This emphasis on the external rather than the internal carried over into many different aspects of life, from beauty advertisements, to the idolization of movie stars, and even in the world of courtship, where the shy, reserved fellow was in danger of being labeled a homosexual, and where the bold flirtatiousness man was "a catch."

Over the years the preference for extroverted characteristics has taken on many different shapes and forms; for example, many educators, psychologists, and social workers, as well as the general public, saw introverted children as individuals who "should be the subject of special care and study, in order to avoid the development of further difficulties." That quote was taken from a journal published in 1922 but, with a little tweaking, the general idea—that introversion should be a cause for concern—fits right in with many modern opinions on the introversion-extroversion trait. Consider the anecdote from above, where both a stranger and my mother expressed concern over my social habits, and compare as well the stereotype of the introverted, creepy loner who sits at the back of the class without ever speaking.

WHAT THE EXTROVERT ADVANTAGE LOOKS LIKE

Charismatic and gregarious individuals who are quick to act and more than willing to take risks are typically seen more favorably than their quieter counterparts. They are the ideal; extroversion is the "dominant" personality type in the sense that extroverted individuals tend to have an advantage over introverts because the world has been shaped to largely suit them. Consider the following:

• Think about how many offices are organized today. Many businesses choose to go with an open-floor plan that gives employees little to no privacy, meaning that the introverted individual is being hit constantly with external stimuli throughout the day. The extrovert, however, thrives off of this.

- How do companies organize their workforce? Most use teams and groups, who hold brainstorming sessions where people just throw out the ideas that pop into their head. Again, this is great for extroverts, who think out loud, but terrible for introverts, who want time to process and fully develop their ideas. If you want good ideas from an introvert, give them some time to think about it, and they'll come back with a list full of them. Ask them to think of something on the spot and they are likely to freeze up.

- Think about the emphasis that universities put on classroom discussions. This is one that has definitely affected me. I remember those discussion-centred classes in college—they were hell. My grades on my tests were near perfect, but I had to work so hard to not lose daily participation points simply because it's not part of my introverted nature to jump in with ideas as part of a larger group. And I never understood how people actually learned in that kind of environment; all of those people just tossing out ideas like beads at Mardi Gras was just too disorganized for me.

THE EFFECTS OF THE EXTROVERT ADVANTAGE

The extrovert advantage has a multitude of repercussions on both the individual and societal level. For example:

- It has given rise to the notion that introversion is a sign of incompleteness. Recall how Cheryl tried to reassure my mother that I would "grow out of it." Much like bedwetting, throwing food, and biting, introversion is a negative trait that will hopefully disappear as one ages.

- It has made extroversion is the default setting; introversion is "the other." Cheryl was not concerned at all for my brother, seeming to regard his behavior as normal, but with one look, she had already started thinking that there was something wrong with me.

- The world is viewed through extroverted-tinted glasses. Consider this: how many people have mistaken your tendency to sit quietly alone as a sign of sadness or depression? It does not occur to extroverts that introverts may find that type of activity enjoyable; they see it as how they would react to it, that is, with feelings of melancholy. Or, for another example, think about how introverts are often written off as cold, aloof, and snobbish because they tend to not chit-chat with others or join in on group activities.

THE INTROVERT'S PLACE IN AN EXTROVERTED WORLD

In the next few chapters, I'm going to talk about how to take on some extrovert characteristics in order to better navigate the extrovert world in which we live. This should not be taken as a call to completely abandon your introverted ways and lie about who you are. The world needs introverts, though they may not realize it.The world cannot be run solely by individuals who act on instinct, think out loud, and try to take charge. That would essentially be a world of Donald Trumps—an incredibly scary thought. Introverts make substantial contributions to the world around them, as long as they are given the chance.

Introverts Excel at Observation and Analyzing

It makes sense, if you think about it. While extroverts are busy talking, the introvert is taking everything in, listening to what is being said, and analyzing all of it. Some introverts are even pretty good at reading people and situations, given their observational skills.

Introverts Recharge

Is your extrovert coworker running out of steam while working late on a project? Unless there's a party or some kind of excitement around, good luck getting anything out of them. The introvert, however, just needs some quiet time alone, away from their work and other people, in order to refresh themselves.

Someone Needs to Be Around to Listen

Introverts make great listeners; without them, extroverts would never have an audience. Also, because introverts tend to be analytical and prefer well thought-out solutions, they are the perfect counterbalance to the extrovert who goes bananas with his brainstorming. Someone has to rein that guy in and tell him that no, we can't manufacture elephant-drawn hot air balloons that function in outer space in order to increase customer interest.

ATTITUDE & APPROACH

Alright, fellow introverts. For this chapter to work, you need to accept two statements as true:

1) In order to achieve your goals, you need to be able to competently navigate social situations from everyday one-on-one interactions to parties, functions, and other large gatherings. In other words, giving into your introverted tendencies is not a viable option if success is desired.

2) These goals are a priority for you, which means you are willing to sacrifice certain other things in order to achieve them, as well as take risks. For our purposes, what you will be sacrificing is your comfort level and what you are risking is failure and perhaps embarrassment (but that could be said for any number of potentially rewarding ventures).

Why do I say this? Because this chapter is all about how to overcome or, at the very least, combat your natural aversion to certain social situations.

PRIORITIES

Your priorities are a major factor in your behavior. We often show what is most important to us through our actions or inactions.

Let's begin with two scenarios:

1) A coworker has been playing "It's a Small World", the song so irritating that it has been banned by the UN as a form of torture, all day long. It is 2:30pm and you have never wanted to smash someone's face and/or computer more. Your fingers keep curling into a fist, just hoping for a reason to end the agony. Do you get up and punch this man and destroy his work computer? No. Why? Because there is something inside your head that reminds you that a) you need your job and breaking a computer is a great way to lose it, b) that punching

a person, no matter how annoying, is usually grounds for an assault charge and you would not do well in prison, and c) he is bigger than and could crush you. It is a sense of self-preservation, an acknowledgement that assuaging your discomfort is not as important as what you are seeking to gain or maintain by keeping your cool.

2) The big company for which you work is throwing a party for all of its employees. You are relatively new and do not know many people. This is a great opportunity to connect with people with whom you will be working closely, and a way to observe and understand the inner workings of this particular corporate machine. However, you are an introvert. The last time you attended a party, you slept for two days and were still exhausted. Plus, you did not find it very enjoyable. Do you go? If you are like most introverts, no, you do not. Why? Because it is not something that you like to do.

How are these two scenarios different? Both involve choices that must be made between ensuring your own comfort and securing, maintaining, or bettering your work life. In the end, it comes down to priorities—if you want to improve your social standing, be considered for more opportunities, or be noticed by certain people, then you must be willing to do the work that such things require. In this case, the "work" that must be done is socializing and you must learn how to make yourself do it.

QUESTIONING YOUR NATURAL RESPONSE

It is important to recognize that our initial reactions to certain situations do not necessarily dictate the best course of action. For example, you may find that your natural response to being invited to a party is to immediately think, "No, no, no, no, no. I hate parties; they're so stressful." and subsequently find yourself coming up with a variety of excuses as to why you cannot attend. This is what may be most comfortable for you, but it certainly isn't helping you achieve your goals.

Be Stern

Even grown adults need a talking-to from a stern-faced voice of reason every once in a while, even if it comes from inside their own heads. Think of it as the sibling to your conscience; instead of telling you what is right and what is wrong, it tells you what is beneficial and what is disadvantageous, what is smart and what is self-defeating. My parents used to tell me, "It doesn't matter what you *want* to do, this is what you *have* to do." and this is essentially what you have to remember to tell yourself when you start thinking of skipping an important social event. Force yourself outside of your comfort zone, even if the responsible adult part of you has to drag you kicking and screaming out of the house.

Remember Your Priorities

If you have a fear of heights and your priority is to overcome it, then going with your natural response to situations involving high places will not help you achieve this goal at all. Instead, you have to remember that you want to conquer this fear and that the only way to do this is by facing it. It is similar with social situations. If your goal is to obtain a promotion or find new friends, remind yourself that you will never get what you want if you don't take certain actions. This seems quite obvious and rational—until you get into the moment and a wave of panic and anxiety hit you and your rational self ceases to be the dominant voice in your head. You may find it helpful to write down your priorities and how to achieve them and keep that list somewhere extremely visible in order to remind yourself of what you want to achieve.

Tell Yourself the Benefits

After my parents would tell me that I *had* to do something, being the impertinent child that I was, I would always ask them why. In most cases, their answer was something like, "Because I told you to, that's why." That kind of response works well on a kid, but as an adult, I have found that grown-up, panicked me requires a little more convincing. Most people set goals because they think that achieving them will reap positive rewards and/or desired outcomes and introverts are no different. Do you remember that little list you made of your priorities and how to achieve them? Now you're going to add another section to it, one that states the reason(s) why you want to meet that goal. Remind yourself of what you stand to gain by doing something that furthers your efforts.

SUCK IT UP AND SMILE

This is a technique that I have deemed the "Suck It Up and Smile" strategy. You can think of it as a more hardcore version of being stern with yourself or the adult version of "because I said so, that's why." In short, you remind yourself that life isn't fair, that sometimes we have to do things that we don't want to do, and that we can either make the best out of it in order to see some kind of benefit or be miserable and gain nothing. This is probably the one that I use the most with myself—what can I say, I was a stubborn little kid and as an adult, nothing much has changed.

SOCIAL PREPARATION

Introverts are known for their tendency to think before speaking or acting. Most will mentally rehearse before a speech, for example, and when a decision needs to be made, introverts are more likely to give the issue careful consideration before making a choice. In other words, an inclination to prepare, rather than rushing off with no plan (the preferred extroverted method of action), is a common characteristic of introverts that is actually extremely helpful for those introverts who want/need to be more social. Additionally, because introverts are not big risk-takers, instead preferring the comfort of the familiar, any amount of preparation will make social situations seem less intimidating; this applies both to daily interpersonal interactions as well as to social engagements or special events or occasions.

FUELING YOUR SOCIAL TANK

Introverts find their energy within themselves and that energy is expended by social situations, much like a car uses fuel. Just as you do not want to start a road trip with your gas tank empty, so too do you not want venture out into the outside world to go to a party or networking event when you are feeling drained and exhausted, either physically or mentally. If horror movies have taught us anything it should be this: failing to fuel up can have disastrous consequences-- everybody knows that the person who breaks down and leaves the safety of the car is usually the first to be horrifically murdered, so keep that in mind when you are preparing for an event. You may not die, but the outcome will almost certainly not be particularly positive. Your goal should be to keep your social fuel tank adequately filled when you know that you are going to be interacting with others. Parties, get-togethers, and other special functions typically require more social fuel than day-to-day interpersonal situations (such as those with family, coworkers, or partners) that tend to be more one-on-one or small-group oriented.

Fueling Up

Out of all of the tips and advice in this book, this is going to be either the easiest or the hardest. Why? Because fueling up simply requires you to engage in activities that you find enjoyable, relaxing, and energizing. Introverts require solitude and time to sink into the depths of their own minds while more or less forgetting about the world around them; if you deny yourself this time, you are basically sabotaging your own efforts at sociability. Now, for some, this may be difficult due to busy schedules, responsibilities (I'm looking at you, introverted parents of toddlers who always look like they are on the verge of tears), and commitments but it is vitally necessary if you want to be able to function at your best.

Identify the activities in which you find pleasure. For many, this could be reading a book, writing, engaging in various artistic pursuits, doing yoga or exercising, or simply sitting back and thinking about something (it doesn't really matter what), but the specific activity matters much less than the effect that it has on your mental state. In other words, go for whatever works best for you. However, I do suggest that the activity you choose be upbeat in nature. Do not watch or read a tear-jerker, do not read the obituaries or stories about abused animals and/or children. Most introverts already view social interaction through a slightly negative lens—there is no need to add to that. You want positivity, so watch a funny movie, watch cat videos on YouTube (a personal favorite), or engage in something else that makes you smile, or, at the very least, that makes you not-sad.

For example, in my own life, I often choose to recharge by coloring while watching a show that I have already seen. I allow myself to become completely absorbed in laying down color, thinking about color palettes, deciding on shading—all of those elements that make coloring fun for me come to the forefront of my mind and dominate it for an extended period of time. I have the television show on for background noise and I purposefully pick a show that I have already watched so that I do not have to pay attention to understand story lines or plot and can instead focus on coloring.

However, many people do not have this kind of time, at least not on a regular basis. Finding "alone time" when this is your situation is understandably difficult, but it can be done. Carve out time in your schedule, even if it is just a few minutes, to re-energize yourself. Obviously, the specifics of this will vary from person to person and depend on an individual's specific situation, but one of the following examples may work for you, either as is or after some tweaking:

- Reading a book, sketching, daydreaming, etc., in the car while you wait in a carpool line or while you are in a waiting room.

- Ducking off somewhere to be alone for lunch, then eating quickly so that you can have more time to devote to your refueling endeavors

- Find solace in the bathroom. Yes, I know it is a strange place to "relax" but think about it—no one is going to open the door and interrupt you or barge in. It is (usually) pretty quiet and still, so take a little extra time to gather yourself.

- Get up a little earlier in the mornings and devote that time to seeing to your own needs as an introvert. You will likely find that the workplace is much more enjoyable, or, at least, tolerable, when you are not permanently miserable.

Just remember: Your ability to successfully navigate through a day filled with social interaction and external stimulation partially depends on your energy level. Do not think of this as an option; if you want to improve your sociability, this is something that you _must_ do.

PICKING YOUR BATTLES

There are going to be days when, no matter how much social fuel you have in your tank, you will neither feel as if you are ready to be social nor will you want to do any socializing. This is okay—it happens to everyone. There are some days when I just _cannot_ deal with people; it is like every bit of extroverted-ness inside me has either left the building or lost its will to live. You can force it, of course, and in many cases you will have to do so because of commitments and responsibilities. However, these days are _not_ when you should be considering going to a party. If you must go, keep it short. Make an appearance, schmooze as much as is appropriate, then disappear mysteriously into the night like you are Batman. It is better to make a good quick first impression than hanging around and totally flubbing it.

GATHER INTEL

Because introverts prefer the familiar, the unknown nature of social interaction, whether it is in the workplace or at a special event, can be a source of anxiety. Generally speaking, introverts are not the people who jump into risky situations and they tend to learn by observing, not by doing. In other words, we like to know what we are getting into before we venture into a new situation. When you are looking familiarize yourself with a specific situation, there are two key questions that you should answer; this should give you enough information to allow you to have a general idea of the kind of environment in which you are entering. The goal for this is to make yourself feel more comfortable and less apprehensive or anxious. For introverts, the only way to not fear the unknown is to…well, know it.

What Kind of Event Is It?

There are a plethora of different types of events to which you may be invited and almost any of them could be casual, semi-formal, or formal. The latter should be kept in mind when picking out your outfit for said event, but the type of event is much more important as it will dictate the kinds of subject matter that are appropriate, what the format will be (for example, it may be a mix-and-mingle affair, or a formal sit-down dinner with assigned seating), and who will be there. Which brings us to our second question:

Who Will Be There?

You may already know this, but if you do not, finding out who the other attendees are can be a great help to you; just talk to the event's organizer and casually inquire as to the types of people who will be there. This way, you can know if the party/event will be full of acquaintances, coworkers, a mix of people from your workplace, friends, people with whom you may have had a previous altercation, etc. Knowing about the guest list can be a great comfort to you if you discover that there will be a lot of people that you already personally know; it can also give you time to prepare if the other partygoers are largely made up of strangers, higher-ups in the company, acquaintances, and the like.

PACK AMMUNITION

Introverts tend to have a few close friends rather than a large circle of acquaintances and we generally prefer deep conversations. Unfortunately, this is not always an option. In order to be socially successful, sometimes you must interact within a group or meet a large number of new people. The latter is particularly true if you are looking to network and establish connections for your career. This means engaging in light conversation and small talk (something we will talk more about in the chapter on verbal communication), but in order to do this successfully, you need to be able to relate to a large number of people on a surface level, at the very least. This is where packing "ammunition" comes into play, except instead of stocking up on bullets, you are loading your brain with information and developing your own personal material.

General Information Gathering

Before you go to an event, read up on pop culture, current events, reviews for new movies and books if you can't get to the theatre or bookstore to see or read them. You should also do a quick study of popular television programs. If you know who the other attendees are and have some idea of their interests, pay special attention to those. This comes in handy at work functions—you may hear your coworkers talking to each other about a certain subject on a regular basis, so take them into account when you are doing your prep work. If you are going to an industry-specific event, brush up on the current trends in that field. Introverts, by nature, feel most comfortable when they can have time to prepare.

Note: Avoid politics and religion. Do not bring these up and if someone else does, find a way to either change the topic or gracefully leave the conversation. These types of discussions either go really well or they are a total disaster. It's usually the latter, so don't risk it.

Getting Personal

Connections are often made when two people give something of themselves to each other, when they become even a little less guarded and share with one another. This does not mean that you need to have an intensive, deep talk therapy session with everyone with whom you wish to network. Actually, this is a place where many introverts have trouble; they generally prefer to have deep conversations with people they know well, rather than having light conversations with a multitude of acquaintances. However, you still need to be personable, which is why it is a good idea to be prepared to talk about yourself, give your opinions, and share your own experiences.

I have found that there are two keys to preparing for more personal conversation. First, develop an opinion about different areas if pop culture, such as television shows (this is why it is important to do a little background research on those things that are currently popular), so that you can participate in discussions or individual conversations that revolve around these topics. Second, prepare some anecdotes. They can either be real or made up, but if you make them up, be sure to write them down so that you do not contradict yourself later. Anecdotes humanize you, making them an especially important tool for introverts who are seen as cold and snotty. Being able to humorously relay a personal event, especially one in which you look silly or just not-perfect, makes others feel closer to you because they know personal information about you. This is an optional tactic, as, generally speaking, many introverts find it easier to make conversations about the other person by asking them questions and responding. Introverts are usually awesome listeners, so they are well-suited to this task.

THE IMPORTANCE OF COMMUNICATION SKILLS

Communication is an integral part of our everyday lives, whether it is verbal or non-verbal and our ability to do so effectively has an incredible impact on almost every aspect of our lives, from the mundane to the life-changing. It is curious, then, that so little attention is paid to it until after we reach adulthood. I have never had to use calculus since graduating from high school, but I must communicate everyday—guess which subject they forced me to take in school? (Spoiler alert: it was calculus. And it was hell.) Perhaps it is because we are so immersed in communication that it seems ridiculous to cover something considered basic—and for some people, this approach (or non-approach) is fine; they automatically pick up on proper communication techniques and the nuances therein without even seeming to think much about it. But for others, the ability to communicate effectively does not come so easily. This puts us at quite a disadvantage because too much depends on proper communication skills for us to continuously flub it or avoid it completely.

This is particularly true for the introvert who desires to improve their social skills, social standing, increase their popularity, or heighten others' opinions of them, to whatever ends. Personal fulfillment, mental well-being, professional success, as well as success in one's personal life with friends, family, acquaintances, and romantic partners all start from one place, and that is social interaction fueled by communication.

A common myth about introverts is that they are, by definition, poor communicators because the traits that characterize introversion are incompatible with the ability to effectively interface with others. This is simply not true; introverts have the potential to communicate just as well as extroverts, and be just as effective at it. Now, are some introverts poor communicators? Of course, but, keep in mind, many extroverts are as well. The prevalence of this myth is largely due to the fact that living in a world where extrovert traits are preferred and seen as the norm means that behavior is just one of the many aspects of life that are interpreted through an extroverted lens. In other words, what an introvert is doing and what an extrovert *perceives* them to be doing are often two totally different things. And this, understandably, causes some problems.

IMPROVING YOUR VERBAL COMMUNICATION

Experts say that the majority of communication is done non-verbally, but when it comes to developing relationships with others verbal communication is key, as it is what most effectively relays our thoughts, interests, ideas, and opinions. In other words, the content of speech is what helps us form connections with others. You can't bond with someone over your shared love of Stephen King novels or communicate complex ideas in a brainstorming session through micro-expressions and gestures alone. (Well, I suppose you could, but that'd mean conversing using charades, which seems a little extreme.) Introverts are often thought to be bad verbal communicators, but that is not a fair assessment. We are quieter than our extroverted counterparts and our methods of communicating are sometimes lost on them, this is true, but this doesn't make us bad verbal communicators. It makes us different. That said, there is no doubt that it can be hard for us to communicate effectively within a world whose default personality type is set to "extrovert", which is what this chapter is about—learning how to bridge the gap between yourself and your peers to foster more effective verbal communication.

STEP OUTSIDE YOUR COMFORT ZONE

Being an introvert in an extroverted world means that more often than not, you are going to be the one who has to make concessions to the other side if you want to be socially successful. It's not very fair and it can be a total pain in the rear, but as we have discussed before, sometimes you have to sacrifice your own comfort in order to achieve your goals. So let's go over the extrovert's preferences regarding verbal communication:

• They tend to think out loud, working out their ideas as they engage in conversations and discussions. In brainstorming sessions, they throw out ideas like a Mardi Gras float tosses out beads.

- They require a lot of stimulation; in-depth one-on-one conversations are not their preference. They prefer talking to multiple people about different topics.

- They enjoy small talk and will often start with that before delving into the topic/s at hand.

In order to be able to effectively communicate with extroverts and other personality types in general, it is imperative that you be accommodating of these and other preferences and be prepared to be flexible in how you communicate.

Interrupting and Being Interrupted

Extroverts like to talk; they have no problem filling your pauses with their own thoughts and they tend to interrupt others, especially when they have their own ideas. As an introvert, you can approach this situation in two ways—you can sit back and wait for your turn to talk or you can join in the conversation and make yourself visible. It can be hard to know when to interrupt, so the next time you are in a group of extroverts, observe how and when they do it, then try it yourself.

When introverts speak, they usually verbalize long, complete thoughts, which is the opposite of the extrovert's unfiltered stream-of-consciousness style, which does not take too long to relay to others. Basically, what I'm saying is that you should be prepared to be interrupted if this is how you choose to communicate. Don't take it personally and don't see it as a signal that the other person doesn't value your opinions and thoughts. Use it as a moment to increase your visibility by calling attention back to yourself and to the fact that you were not done speaking. Using humor in these situations can help to break any tension that may arise.

Push Yourself Outside of Your Head

Introverts like their thoughts to be fully developed before they voice them to others, but this does not always mesh with rapid fire brainstorming sessions and other similar workplace situations. You may be concocting some brilliant ideas, but no one else can see inside your head. You don't get credit for what you don't share; good ideas go to waste if they stay inside your head. So, instead of working out every little detail of a thought inside your own head before you relay it to a colleague or group, release that thought into the wild and let your peers pounce on it, change it, add to it, bounce off of it, and work it out together as a group. Yes, doing so will probably go against your nature and I will be the first one to admit that it feels extremely weird when you first start doing it, but the more you do it, the more natural it will become. Similarly, when a colleague presents his or her own ideas, join in on the discussion and pipe up with your own opinions, recommendations, and thoughts, even if you haven't had a chance to fully evaluate them. It's okay if an idea does not work; just toss it out and keep thinking and making suggestions. Introverts tend to obsess over tiny details; you may find it helpful to practice thinking more "big picture".

SMALL TALK

Small talk and chit-chat might as well be foreign languages to many introverts, but, like all languages, it can be learned, developed, and perfected. Many introverts, myself included, see small talk as pointless conversation that is shallow, superficial, and therefore not worth their time. This is not true; shockingly, small talk does have a purpose and it is actually incredibly important, especially for the introvert looking to improve their social skills and have more success in their interpersonal relationships. Small talk is where you start—before you can have a deep conversation with someone, you must begin with the basics. Small talk is how you find common ground with your conversation partner and establishes an initial connection.

Small Talk in Action

Granted, a question like, "How was your weekend?" can seem pretty pointless (especially if you do not particularly care about the answer), but think of it as the gateway to a more interesting conversation. Listen closely to what they say, maintaining eye contact, and look for mentions of possible topics that may represent points of coinciding interests or, at the very least, a topic about which you know and can expand upon. Most introverts prefer deeper conversation to chit-chat, but in order to have an exchange like that, you must first get the irksome fluff out of the way. Let's take a look at a sample situation—a conversation between Steve, an introvert, and Jason, his colleague.

> *Steve:* How was your weekend?

> *Jason:* Oh, it wasn't too bad. We went hiking Saturday because of the nice weather, but Sunday I just bummed around and binge-watched *Archer*.

There are several places we can go from here; Jason has given us plenty of information with which to work. Steve could ask about the hiking trip, agree about the weather and share something he did, or talk about *Archer*, a television show he enjoys. In this case, he picks hiking.

> *S:* Oh, hiking sounds fun! Where did you go?

> *J:* Just to Mount Vader—we had the kids with us and it's an easy trail for their little legs. They're starting to get too heavy to carry.

Bingo. Steve struck gold when Jason mentioned his family. Conversing about a topic that has some kind of emotional hold over the other person gets them more involved in the conversation while making you look like a caring, pleasant individual. When talking to a parent, kids are usually a safe topic to broach, especially if you know that they are proud of their child's accomplishments. Steve continues:

> *S:* Oh, you have kids? How many?

> *J:* We have two—Rubella is eight and Cholera is nine. They're in the same class though, Rubella skipped first grade.

Jason has an intelligent daughter and he seems particularly proud of her. Alright, Steve, take it away:

> *S:* Wow, that's really impressive; you must be so proud of her. Are they in the same class?

And so on and so on. Steve did several things right in this situation: he asked questions, maintained (or feigned) interest, and looked for opportunities to increase the conversation's depth. He survived chit-chatting and he barely had to speak—he just had to actively listen and go from there. Will things always go this smoothly? Of course not, but everyone has their socially awkward moments, even extroverts. Let's look at one more example, this time assuming that Steve decided to pick Jason's binge-watching of *Archer* as his point of interest.

> **Steve:** That's such a great show! How many seasons did you get through?

>> **Jason:** All of them—I did nothing else the entire day. It's my favorite show, so I do that every once in a while.

>> **S:** It's so easy to get caught up in it. Which season do you think was the best?

>> **J:** Hmm…I really enjoyed season five, I think. That's my favorite.

>> **S:** It's mine as well. I wished they had brought back Cherlene as a character in season six; everything she did was just amazing.

>> **J:** Season six wasn't too bad though. I'm enjoying watching Archer try to be a father.

>> **S:** Haha, he's trying so hard in his…Archer-ish way. You know, I've really enjoyed his character arc a lot more than I thought I would.

>> **J:** I think my favorite is learning more and more about Cheryl—she's just freaking crazy.

>> **S:** I think Cheryl has the best quotes in the show. "Hey, will you choke me a little bit?" still gets me every time.

In this scenario, Steve chose to talk more about a subject that he and Jason had in common—their love of the television show, *Archer*.

What followed was a pretty intense fanboy session that allowed the two to bond. Will they become best friends? Probably not, but now Steve will always have something to talk to Jason about; in time, he may stumble upon other shared interests, but *Archer* has laid the foundation.

Notice the difference between the two Steves. In the first conversation, Steve plays a largely passive role, asking questions and absorbing information, but sharing none of his own. In the second situation, Steve is much more enthusiastic, contributing equally to the conversation once it has reached a subject he enjoys. Both are acceptable approaches, but the latter leaves a more lasting impression.

TRY TO CONTROL YOUR ENVIRONMENT

Noisy, bustling environments are not particularly introvert-friendly, as they tend to quickly sap our energy, overwhelm us, and cause us to stress. If you already have trouble verbally communicating, or if you are unsure of your ability to do so effectively, it is in your best interest to try and make sure that your interactions with other people occur in environments in which you are comfortable. It is unlikely that you will always be able to have total control over when and where you converse with others, in which case, you will have to improvise and do what you can to shape the environment to your advantage.

Controlling the Environment

Scheduled meetings, whether they are with work colleagues, bosses, potential romantic partners, and acquaintances, are an introvert's best friend when it comes to social engagements. Not only do you have time to prepare yourself for being social, but you can have greater influence over the location at which said interaction is to take place by recommending a spot that is quiet and calm and, if possible, one that you find comforting.

Personal Dates

For example, if you are arranging a date with a new acquaintance, try to meet up at a place where you can have some one-on-one time in order to establish an initial connection that, hopefully, will put you at ease. If they suggest meeting at a bar at a time when it is always busy, counter with an idea that is similar in nature, but more introvert-friendly. For instance, you can suggest that the two of you meet at the same location, but at a time when it is less busy, or recommend a quieter location, such as a small coffee shop or a less-popular bar.

Work meetings

Controlling the location of a meeting for work is a bit more difficult because your options can be limited, depending on the person with whom you are meeting, the nature of the conversation, and office protocol. Informal meet-ups are usually easiest to handle. For instance, if you are meeting with a work colleague in order to brainstorm, solve a minor problem, or confirm or relay information, suggest that the two of you meet in the workspace that, between the two of you, is the most conducive to conversation. If your workplace has spare meeting rooms or offices, you can try to arrange the use of one of those. In the case that the location must be a specific place, request that you meet at a time when the area is the calmest and quietest; perhaps you can arrange to get to work a little earlier than usual before your fellow workers arrive, or to stay later than usual.

For more formal meetings, such as those that take place with bosses or with a team, your options are more limited. When it comes to meeting with your superior, try to make use of their office, especially if it is in a quiet area or if there is a way to block out other noise and activity. If they are not amenable to that, or if they do not have an office, suggest the spaces and times in which you would have an informal one-on-one meeting. With team meetings, suggest that the group congregate in an enclosed space that is either not surrounded by noise or built in such a way as to block out sound. Because these can involve large groups or special equipment, you may just have to deal with the best less-than-ideal location. What you absolutely do not want is for the meeting to be held in a common area, so try to steer the group away from those places as best as you can.

Improvising

Of course, you can't schedule every social interaction that you have throughout the day. People may pop in to your office or workspace in order to ask a question, they may strike up a conversation at lunch, or they may approach you in a common area. If these places are not busy and loud, then, in most cases, they should not cause you much difficulty. If those are busy areas, then, when the person or people approach you, before you get too involved in the conversation, suggest a change in time or location. Say something like, "Perhaps we can step into the hall.", or "Why don't we talk in the break room?". Be polite and friendly and try to not sound like you are panicking because of the sudden social interaction. Maintain eye contact, consider giving them a nod to show that you acknowledge them and are paying attention, and when you make a suggestion, say it with a warm smile and don't be demanding. Introverts often garner a reputation for being cold and snooty, making it hard to work with others, so you want to do your best to come across as friendly and communicative, not withdrawn and detached.

Give Your Reasons

I think we can all agree that, depending on how it is said, a request to meet somewhere private can come across as ominous or creepy. When you make such a suggestion, take on a relaxed, confident tone and try to not make it sound like a big deal. Check out the following examples:

Work Situations

At your job, you want to come across as someone with whom it is easy to work. Therefore, it is in your best interest to not come across as persnickety and neurotic, so when you suggest a change in environment, give a reason that makes it sound like it would be beneficial for all parties involved.

Them: "Hey, I was wondering if we could go over that report you filed on the growth of militant livestock movements."

You: "Of course, no problem. It's a rather delicate matter, though, so why don't we step into the hallway for a minute and I'll fill you in. I think you'll find the statistics on the participation of cows in acts of arson *udder-ly* fascinating." (Yes, it's a bad pun, but you get the idea— inject a little humor if it is appropriate or acceptable.)

Them: "We should probably get together and come up with some ideas before tomorrow's meeting, what do you think?

You: "Sounds like a good idea. Do you have plans for lunch? We can use the meeting room down the hall and see what we can bang out. The break room just gets so noisy, it's hard to hear anyone in there."

Social Occasions

When it comes to arranging dates or meetings with acquaintances, you can make the reasoning behind the suggestion about you. After all, you want to present a clear picture of yourself and this is a part of your personality.

Them: "About our date. I was thinking we could hit that bar down the street."

You: "That'd be great. Do you mind meeting me at the park across the street? It's really hard to find anyone in there."

Them: "Any ideas for what you want to do tonight?"

You: "There's a really great coffee shop close by—would you like to meet there and hang out for a while? I'd love to be able to talk with you some more."

ALLOW YOURSELF TIME TO THINK

Introverts tend to contemplate before speaking, which can seem like a disadvantage during conversations. Indeed, it can make us feel rushed, nervous, and ill-prepared, especially next to our extroverted colleagues who navigate conversations with ease as they think out loud. I think we all know that conversing with someone when you feel harried and anxious rarely turns out very well, but the nature of verbal communication seems to demand that introverts put themselves into situations in which those feelings are inevitable. That can be true—if you let it. But you do not have to do so; you can bend the rules of normal conversational etiquette to make the experience more introvert friendly.

While it is usually not considered proper to lapse into silence during a conversation, it is acceptable to buy yourself some time by telling the other person or people that you need a minute to think in order to give them the best answer or ideas. When you find that you need time for your thoughts to catch up with the conversation, say something like "Give me a moment, let me think about this." or "I want to make sure I explain this properly, so give me just a second." When you allow yourself the time you need to think through a topic or question, you can usually come up with better answers and ideas than you would have if you had tried to talk and think the extrovert way. You may garner a reputation for being slow to speak, but provided that the content of your words is of high-quality, you can also develop a reputation as a thoughtful and insightful individual that can be depended upon for good ideas and solutions.

Before you use this tactic, however, there are two things you need to keep in mind—

- If you ask for time to think so that you can give your conversation partner/s a decent response, you need to make sure that you deliver. In other words, if you take a moment to gather yourself, making others wait on you, and you come up with nothing, then you reap no benefits and if it happens often, you may see a decline in your reputation.

- You cannot constantly ask for time to think. Practice being able to think quickly and pay attention to the direction of the conversation so that you can be ready to speak when spoken to. Try to process the information as quickly as possible; you want to be respectful of the other person's time. Save this tactic for complex questions and thoughts.

ASK QUESTIONS

Introverts tend to be good listeners, which is great because a majority of people like to talk about themselves and will do so if given the opportunity. Introverts like to talk about themselves too; we just prefer to do it with a small number of people on a deeper level. Plus, it can be hard for us to establish that initial connection with someone, which goes back to the purpose of small talk. Therefore, harnessing our natural inclination to sit back, take in our surroundings, and think lends itself nicely to focusing the conversation on the other person, taking you out of the spotlight. You can do this by asking them questions, actively listening to their answers, responding appropriately, and inquiring further. Don't make it like a rapid-fire question-and-answer session; it needs to be more conversational and personable than that.

Not only does asking questions keep the focus of the conversation off of you, it also builds up the relationship between the two of you. As you question and they answer and you respond, you are both learning about each other and, hopefully, making a positive impression. Plus, everyone likes a good, friendly listener. As long as you share a little of yourself in the process, you can develop a reputation for being someone who cares about others and isn't self-centered, but who is friendly and has an interesting personality as well. This initial interaction can be the doorway to a deeper friendship, better working relationship, or a romantic relationship.

NONVERBAL COMMUNICATION

Scientific research has shown that, on average, extroverts are better at decoding nonverbal cues and more confident in their abilities to do so than introverts. The reason(s) for this are not completely known, though a large part of it may be due to the fact that extraverts simply have more experience interacting with people, as they seek it out in order to satisfy their desire for external stimulation. Introverts, on the other hand, do not do this, making us less experienced. There is a second component to this—introverts do not physically express their emotions as clearly as most extroverts. Because we tend to not think about the external, we do not consider our body's positioning in relation to our mood; we may be feeling super happy, but our body language is giving off a completely different signal. This is a common cause of miscommunications and misjudgments, both of which can have lasting consequences. The good news is that communication skills, both verbal and nonverbal, are learned behaviors. You may not think of yourself as a good communicator, but with enough knowledge and practice, you can be.

PERSONAL SPACE

Put your arms out to the side. Imagine that they are the diameter of a circle, creating a space in which you are the center. This is your bubble. Everyone has their own personal bubble and it is important to respect that whenever possible. Now, there are some situations in which this is not feasible, like on a crowded train or a packed concert. But, as a general rule you want to stand no closer to someone than an arm length. (Of course, as you get closer to someone it may become okay to move in, but when you're starting out, give them room to breathe. Hovering over someone or getting extremely close to them can be threatening, creepy, or just plain uncomfortable. Standing too far away shows disinterest, or perhaps a lack of confidence.

The amount of personal space that an individual needs varies from person to person. The arm-length rule is a good basic scale, but you'll probably meet people who don't mind standing closer and you'll definitely meet people who have no concept of personal space at all.

Personal Space and Gender Issues

Now, a lesson that tends to apply more for the men who want to talk to women than it does for women. Many, if not most, women are guarded around men, especially those that are more physically imposing. This is not without reason—sexual violence is a problem of which they are very well aware. If they have not been directly affected by it, then there is a good chance that they know someone who has, and if they read the news, they are definitely aware. They should not have to feel this way, but it's an unfortunate reality. It does not matter if you would never commit such an act, the fact is that you are a stranger and they don't know if you are harmless or not, so do not take it personally if they seem a little physically standoffish, or even hesitant about engaging with you. In fact, if you want to blame someone, blame the guys committing acts of violence and harassment since they are the ones who have ruined it for you. Stay at an appropriate distance and look for other nonverbal cues that will tell you how she is feeling. (We'll cover these shortly)

Personal Space and the Workplace

One of the traits complained about most often when it comes to coworker behavior is a tendency to intrude on personal space. (I'm not kidding. Go Google "annoying coworker behavior" or "annoying coworker trait" and see how many lists and rant post results that it brings up.) There are many different reasons as to why this specific behavior is so irritating, but some include:

- The intruding individual has a noxious odor; it can be their breath, their lack of personal hygiene, the presence of too much cologne or perfume, or just their natural body odor.

- They talk too loud.

- They use their bodily presence to behave threateningly, either subconsciously, consciously, or accidentally.

Depending on where you work, repeated violations of personal space could be considered bullying or harassment, so it's always smart to play it safe.

Reading Personal Space Body Language

The rules that apply to your body language also apply to others, and that includes how they take up their own space. If you see someone lurking in a corner, with their arms crossed and feet together, then they are probably uncomfortable or lack confidence, so approach them with that in mind. Make sure to maintain the appropriate arm-length distance in between the two of you, especially at first, as you do not want to make them feel threatened or vulnerable.

Signs that someone is feeling uncomfortable around you include the following:

- Blocking: Putting an object between oneself and another person

- Withdrawing: Increasing the distance between conversation partners. In real life, this can look like someone preparing to run away as if they were in a slasher film.

- Neck/face touching and rubbing: The neck and the face both contain many nerve endings that, when stimulated, cause the heart rate to drop and decreases anxiety. Doing this while in a conversation often shows that the person is nervous and trying to calm down.

- Eye contact: Uncomfortable people will often refrain from making extended eye contact. Please note that no one is able to maintain eye contact with the same person constantly, but when their eyes shift, they should return to looking at you very shortly.

- Feet that are pointed away: Feet that do not face their owner's conversation partner is a strong indicator that they would rather be somewhere else. The major exception to this is if it is not comfortable to have feet that face towards the person with whom one is speaking, such as on a roller coaster or airplane.

It should go without saying that if you want to look like you are comfortable, do not have your nonverbal communication saying the opposite due to your body language. Pay attention to how you posture yourself.

CONFIDENCE

Confidence is one of the most attractive traits a person can have and manifesting its nonverbal cues can not only make you appear confident to others, it can help you to feel more confident as well. Learning to embody confidence is essential, as it shows, among other things, that you have faith in yourself. You may not have confidence now—that's okay. This is one of those cases where "fake it until you make it" is definitely an applicable piece of advice.

Take Up Space

Confident people are not afraid to be physically present. As introverts, we tend to shrink up in public spaces. We don't want too much attention or too much interaction, but as we have discussed, those things are often necessary and they need to be done well. So, when you are in a social situation that matters to you, take up space. Don't shrink up your neck, tuck in your shoulders, fold your arms, or sit with your legs crossed or squeezed so tightly together they could double as a nutcracker. Loosen up. Hold your head up high and keep your neck extended and your chin up. Let your shoulders fall to their natural position and keep your arms to your side (do not cross them). If your natural position in public is scrunched up, this may take some practice, so be mindful of your body's position and alter it, even if it feels a little weird.

Avoid Your Pockets

Displaying your hands is a sign of confidence and can also make you appear to be trustworthy because you look like you have nothing to hide. If having your hands dangling is uncomfortable, stand with your hands on your hips—this keeps your hands close to you, but exudes much more confidence.

Do Not Fidget

Fidgeting and squirming around while talking to someone makes you look uncomfortable and nervous. Don't sit stone-still like a marble statue; that is almost just as bad as squirming because it makes you look as if you are petrified with fear, like a woodland critter stuck in the middle of a busy interstate. You can move around (gestures are an important part of nonverbal communication), but those movements need to be intentional.

Constantly checking your phone is the new fidgeting, so try to avoid doing this. Not only does it make you look like you are nervous, but to check your phone, you must assume a defensive posture—head down, no eye contact, with your arms in front of you. Also, no one wants to engage with a person who is buried in their phone, so put it away.

Firm Handshake

A firm handshake is one of the first nonverbal markers of confidence. Don't be the person who offers someone a dead fish (limp and timid) handshake; grip their hand firmly while keeping your head up and maintaining eye contact. Be sure not to get over zealous—a handshake should be firm, but it is not a hand-crushing contest. If you want feedback on your handshake, practice with a friend.

Smile

A smile can do several things for you. It not only makes you look happy, pleasant, and approachable, but it makes you appear confident as well. This is because it is a sign that you are feeling carefree and have nothing to worry about because you are in total control, totally awesome, and totally know it.

No Crossed Arms

Crossed arms are a defensive pose. Assuming this position makes you look worried and guarded (as if you are scared and need protection from something). Uncrossing them and letting them hang naturally gives off an aura of fearlessness and, of course, confident. It also makes you appear friendlier, more open to others, and more approachable, which are all things you want when you are trying to establish interpersonal connections.

FACIAL EXPRESSIONS

The face is the window to the soul. It's cheesy, but it's almost always true, as it is harder to control the minute changes in our facial muscles as they react to certain situations. Studies have shown that facial expressions are universal; that is, that people all over the world tend to make the same kinds of faces in when they react to the same situations. For example, the way an American's face shows fear will be just like the face of a fearful person living in Siberia. This is actually a really good thing for introverts because they are easy to learn, which is important because introverts often have issues making their inside feelings apparent on their faces.

The Basic Facial Expressions

Not only are facial expressions universal in meaning, there are also a limited number of them. Of course, they may be tweaked given the complexity of human emotion, but scientists have identified a varying number of basic facial expressions. We'll go through seven of them here.

Anger

An angry facial expression is characterized by one or more of the following: bulging or narrowed eyes, lips pressed tightly together, both vertically and horizontally, lips pressed upward, a pushed out jaw, flared nostrils, and lowered eyebrows. If an individual is trying to be menacing while being angry, they may bare their teeth.

Contempt

Contempt is often combined with other emotions, such as anger or disgust, and some scientists do not include it on their lists. I've included it here because introverts are so often judged as having a contemptuous or judgmental look. Contempt is largely characterized by the pulling of one's mouth to the side of the face.

Disgust

Disgust. It's the face you make when you smell sewage or pass a paper mill. People typically show their disgust by wrinkling their nose, pulling up their upper lip, but overall, letting the lips remain loose, and pulling down their eyebrows. They may also lean back or pull their head back.

Fear

When someone shows fear, their eyebrows will often be pulled up and towards each other, eyes may be wide with the upper eyelids raised, and the mouth will be stretched.

Joy

This is an easy one to recognize. The corners of the lips will be pulled up diagonally (a smile, basically), cheeks are raised and there are wrinkles around the eyes, the muscles around which will be tightened.

Sadness

"Droopy" is a good way to describe this emotion's overall look. The corners of the mouth will turned down, the eyes downcast and the eyelids loose, and the inner part of the eyebrows will be raised. If someone is pouting, then they may also jut their lower lip out.

Surprise

Surprise is probably one of the easiest facial expression to distinguish because the change is often so dramatic. The eyebrows are raised curved, there are horizontal wrinkles on the forehead, eyes are wide open, and the jaw drops, but does not stretch.

Introverts and Their Facial Expression

This used to happen to me all the time: I'd be sitting somewhere, usually at school, and be lost in my own head, thinking about random subjects and ideas when one of my friends would come up to me and me why I was angry/upset or just inquire, "What's wrong with you?" Nothing was wrong. I was perfectly happy. And my situation is not uncommon; in fact, many, if not most, introverts have been accused of or thought to be in a negative mood when they are not. A lot of introverts have what is colloquially called a "resting bitch face", meaning that the way our face naturally falls makes us look like we want the world to burn. We may furrow our brows, let our lips go straight or slightly droop them into a frown, and we may "glare" or, as we would call it, simply staring off into space.

This presents a problem for introverts because it makes many others think that we are judging them, or that we are being judgmental. My friends at college used to call it my "eat shit and die" face, jokingly, because they knew that was (usually) the last thing from my mind. Because introverts do not always display the corresponding facial expression for the emotion that they either want to project or are actually feeling, we are often thought to be aloof, cold, angry, and judgmental and, therefore, unapproachable. When they think this, it makes them less likely to want to engage with us in conversation. In the workplace, it can have an incredibly irritating effect and saddle us with a reputation for being "angry" or "unfriendly", even if very few people have actually interacted with us. Socially, it can limit your prospects with potential friends and partners.

GESTURES

The worst plane ride I ever had occurred when I was flying back to college after a break when I was seated next to man who was probably in his sixties. Next to him was either a friend or a stranger he had engaged in conversation. And it was an enthusiastic conversation; the man next to me was gesticulating wildly throughout the flight, whacking me in the head several times. This shows us a couple of things:

1) Gestures can denote the type of conversation being had. In this case, it was a passionate one, obviously about a subject my seat neighbor felt strongly about.

2) The use of gestures requires a happy medium between "none at all" and "haphazardly flailing arms."

In other words, gestures can be extremely effective in relaying your point to another person or group, but must be used responsibly. Now, introverts in public spaces are not typically the types to gesticulate because we tend to keep our bodies scrunched but I'm going to assume that you read the pages immediately preceding this one and now know that you should let body hang loose and take up space. Now, there a lot of different gestures and we don't have the space to cover most of them. Instead, we are going to discuss a few key gestures that can

Nodding

As an introvert, you may find it hard to speak up in conversations, especially with someone with whom you are not familiar. We've discussed previously the importance of asking questions, but for this to be effective, you have to look as if you are engaged with the person and care about their answer. Nodding is a signal that you are paying attention and understand what they are saying. It encourages them to continue speaking too, which takes some of the pressure off of you. My favorite iteration of this is the triple-nod, which is when you nod three times in rapid succession. It shows eagerness and enthusiasm (don't get crazy with the nod, you don't need to totally bend your neck; a few slight dips of the head is enough. You don't want to look like a bobblehead doll.), as well as ongoing interest in what the person has to say.

Related gestures are head shaking, which signifies disagreement or disbelief, and head tilting, which is a sign of submission (it leaves the neck and throat exposed) that makes you look non-threatening and smaller. It can also denote confusion.

Hands-On-Hips

This is a very confident pose. Putting your hands on your hips makes you look larger and allows you to take up more space, two things that are essential if you want to exude confidence.

Hand Gestures for Emphasis

You might have noticed that your extroverted colleagues use a lot of hand gestures when they talk, providing a nonverbal illustration of what they are saying, what they find most important, and/or how they feel about the subject on which they are speaking. You could already use an appropriate amount of hand gesturing during conversations and just not realize it. Film yourself while talking on the phone; you might be surprised at what you are doing subconsciously.

Rules for Using Hand Gestures

Hand gesturing (and gesturing in general) is incredibly complex. Most extroverts and many introverts naturally pick up how to use hand gestures appropriately and when to use them, so it seems like it should be easy. However, for those that must learn them through study, it is much more difficult because of all of the nuances that go along with it. Here are some basic rules to keep in mind when practicing your hand gestures.

- Avoid arm flailing: Using too many gestures or making them too dramatic causes you to look more like a crazy person and less like an effective communicator. It's really hard to take a person seriously, or even be able to concentrate on what they are saying, when they are flapping around like an over-enthusiastic bird.

- Use them with purpose: This goes with the "avoid arm flailing" rule. Instead of constantly gesticulating wildly, only use hand gestures for things of importance, such as when you want to emphasize a certain point or fact. For example, if you are telling someone that you went fishing and caught a really big fish, you should not illustrate this by moving your hand like a fish, miming catching it (the rod-and-reel routine), and then using your hands to denote its amazing size. You should only use it to show the size of the fish, as it is the most important part of the sentence.

- Make it smooth: Hand gestures should be fluid and natural, not jerky. Not only is this less distracting and more appealing, it is also a sign of confidence and makes you look more polished.

- Be aware of cultural differences: Hand gestures are not universal in their meanings; they can vary depending on the culture. If you are going to an unfamiliar area, especially one that is outside of your own country, take a minute to see what their hand gestures denote. You don't want to end up saying something that you did not intend to say.

- Be in sync: The actual content of your speech should match the type of hand gestures that you use. For example, when something is not okay, do not give the thumbs-up sign. This should go without saying, but making this mistake just gets confusing and frustrating for everyone involved, so make sure that you pay attention to what you are doing with your hands and what is actually coming out of your mouth.

- Mimic, with variation: Observe how the person or people with whom you are conversing are gesturing and adopt them yourself, but do not copy them exactly. Change them up just a little bit while still keeping them very similar.

LOOKING MORE APPROACHABLE

Now, we put all of this information together to create a you that looks inviting and approachable or, at the very least, not terrifying and angry.

Practice Your Facial Expressions

This will make you feel a little silly, but it works. Read through the list of facial expressions and their markers (and be free to take cues from television and movies and watch those characters' expressions) and mimic them in front of a mirror. Practice making a happy face, a sad face, a surprised face—you get it. The key here is that you don't want to overdo it. Very few people sit at their work cubicle with a giant smile across their face and most adults do not comically droop their head when they are sad. So you also want to make sure you work on making them a little subtler.

After you practice making those expressions, work on displaying the emotion that you want to project throughout the day. Make yourself remember to smile a little, or to move your eyebrows. You also want your face to show that you are interested in what the other person has to say, so maintain eye contact and make your face react appropriately to their statements.

At Work: An Example

Let's say that people at work think you are angry, judgmental, or find you intimidating. A few changes in body language can really help change your image. Loosen up your body. Don't sit as stiffly in your chair and do not cross your arms—let yourself relax. If, like me, you tend to super-focus on your task and squint your eyes and twist your mouth, widen your eyes a little to make them look less severe and loosen your eyebrows. Stop every once in a while to look around the room; you want to seem as if you are engaged in the world around you, instead of looking like you are stuck up and snobby (another common misconception). Now, you don't want to have a psychotic grin on your face, but try to keep the corners of your mouth slightly up turned—not enough to show your teeth, but enough to look like you're not angry. When engaging with other people, maintain eye contact, keep your voice at a tone that displays confidence, have straight posture, and gesticulate when appropriate.

To make yourself feel more comfortable, try these tactics out on a friendly coworker before using them on strangers.

INTROVERTS IN THE WORKPLACE

Throughout this book, I've talked a lot about tactics to try in the workplace, but there are some topics that are largely workplace specific. That is what we will be covering in this final chapter.

THRIVING IN THE WORKPLACE

For many introverts, the workplace can seem unfriendly and overwhelming and, depending on your coworkers and company culture, fairly irritating. However, with a little bit of work and communication, introverts can and do thrive in their career.

Know Your Strengths

If you are an introvert who hates talking on the phone, don't take a job as a receptionist unless you're sure that you can work through your aversion to phone conversations. Similarly, if you tend to not like to initiate interactions with strangers, do not take a job as a door-to-door salesman. When you take a job, you should do so knowing what is expected of you; if it requires a gregarious personality and you neither have one nor can fake one effectively, you can't take the job and then expect to not have to meet the required standards.

Introverts, and people in general, perform best when their job is one that requires the sort of temperament that they already possess. So, when you go job-hunting or when you are at work, make your strengths known and display them. For example, if you excel at written communication, be sure to write emails that reflect this. If you happen to be a good researcher, make sure every report or document that you submit shows your commitment to detail in its overall thoroughness. Playing to your strengths, showing them off, and getting them noticed is how to garner a reputation for that trait, as well as how to get more of that kind of work. It can also tell your coworkers a little about your temperament, so that you do not have to use introversion as an excuse.

Go Outside of Your Comfort Zone

We have already discussed this in previous chapters, but it's worth another mention. If you find yourself being constantly overlooked or feel as if you have an unfair reputation, don't wait for someone to notice you or for their opinion to change—initiate it yourself. Prepare before meetings and psyche yourself up (and make sure that your social fuel tank is full). Take a deep breath and, during the meeting or brainstorming session, speak up and don't let others talk over you. Demand attention. You can start small with this; make it a goal for you to speak up at least once in your next group meeting. Make it twice for the next time, and so on. It's okay to take baby steps

As for clearing up misconceptions about your personality and temperament, you must first know how other people perceive you. Once you have that figured out, start working on ways in which you can prove them wrong. If others think you are snotty, force yourself to make small talk and general conversations with more people, particularly those around you. If they say that you have no personality, let more of your character shine through in your interpersonal interactions. Also, never underestimate the power of humor and a smile—both can do a lot to combat a reputation of being standoffish, cold, humorless, etc.

INTROVERTS IN LEADERSHIP ROLES

You may think that being an introvert automatically makes you unfit for leadership, or, perhaps, you think/know you would be a good leader, but no one will give you the chance. There is an image that we have when we think of leaders; they are take-charge people who have a commanding presence and don't mind giving orders. In other words, they are extroverts. However, introverts also have many qualities that make them well-suited for leadership roles.

Good Listeners

An extroverted leader may burst in and dominate a room with his steady stream of ideas or with opinions on the ideas of others. They may also talk over others and interrupt. Introverts tend to be just the opposite. They are more than willing to sit back and listen to the ideas of their coworkers, analyzing them as they hear more about them. An introverted leader can guide the group to looking critically at ideas in order to separate the good from the bad. Their willingness to listen to others and allow them plenty of time to speak is something that the rest of the team would prefer, rather than being talked over or ignored. This also gives other introverts in the group a more comfortable environment in which to express themselves, as it is much less overwhelming.

Enjoy Solitude

Put an extrovert in a room in order to sift through documents, or to spend time researching, reflecting, analyzing, writing, envisioning, etc., and they will quickly fizzle out because of the lack of stimulation. Introverts, however, thrive in such environments, and are ideal leaders for projects that require a great attention to detail, a lot of research, and creative thinking. Working in an environment like this and doing these types of tasks actually energizes introverts.

Encourage Depth

Extroverts may be able to throw out ideas at lightning speed, but when it comes to fine-tuning and analyzing those ideas, they do not have much patience. They are more "big picture thinkers" and focusing on one particular thing for too long is hard for them. Introverts prefer to dig deep on specific topics and will generally be able to ask the right questions and have the patience to consider a variety of possibilities in order to determine the best course of action. The work generated by an introvert will, in theory, be meticulous and well thought-out, not a vague and hare-brained jumble of possible good ideas.

INTERVIEW TIPS FOR INTROVERTS

Extroverts (at least most of them) seem to be perfectly comfortable with interviews. They're gregarious by nature, they like to talk, especially about themselves, appear confident and quick-thinking, and because of this, it is easier for them to make a good impression and "sell" themselves to their prospective employer. (Of course, whether or not they are actually competent is irrelevant; I'm sure we've all worked with at least one extroverted individual who was all charisma and no substance, like a mozzarella stick with no cheese, only breading) Since employers are always looking for "go-getters", "self-starters", "team players", and all of those other buzzwords that are basically code for "extrovert", it isn't surprising that interviewers are more likely to hire people who seem to embody those characteristics.

This puts introverts in a tough position. We may be just as smart, just as capable, and as good of a worker as our extroverted peers, but our problem lies in making that initial sale of ourselves during the interview process. Job interviews seem to combine all of those things that introverts hate—making small talk, engaging in shallow conversation, unfamiliar public environments, and speaking with strangers, all while having very little time to process and think through our responses to their questions and statements. In other words, interviews can be an introvert's worst nightmare. For me, personally, they go beyond a normal nightmare—instead I feel as if I've been thrown into the deepest pits of hell and left to roast and die. Even after all of my work studying personality and behavior, I still hate them to this day, and I doubt that will change. However, I have discovered several little tips that, when implemented can make the entire thing much easier with a greater chance of success.

PREPARE, PREPARE, PREPARE

Gather Intel

As introverts, we may not be great in situations that require "on-the-fly" skills, but we excel at preparation and research, so you want to use these skills to your advantage. Look up any information you can on the company with which you are applying. This means poring over their company website, familiarizing yourself with their management structure and their current executives, studying their competitors, reading any articles that mention either your prospective employer or other businesses, and making sure that you thoroughly understand the industry and its current performance. Also, if possible, look up all information on the person with whom you will be interviewing; learn where they went to school, what they've said in the press, if they belong to any organizations—anything and everything. This is quite similar to preparation for parties and other social engagements, except in this case, you'll likely be looking up information that is much more technical in nature.

Practice

During your intel gathering, you're sure to discover what kind of traits and skills the industry or company requires and what kind of people they are looking for. You should also make it a point to go over what the standard interview questions are. Consider what you are most likely to be asked by your interviewer and practice your answers ahead of time You should also see if you can enlist a friend or family member into helping you by getting them to play the part of the interviewer and having them ask you questions. This way, you can get some honest feedback on how you sound, how you look, and what you need to improve.

Of course, well-practiced answers will only get you so far. You don't want to sound like a robot; you want to be seen as a creative, talented, and special individual. For this, I recommend bringing in a portfolio (if you have one) and a pad and pen. Before the interview, jot down some key words and phrases that can serve as prompts to help you remember the points you want to make and the information that you want to emphasize. That way, if you happen to lose your train of thought, you can casually look down, see the information, and regain your footing. Remember: your goal here is to sell yourself, so it's smart to have a concise list of those "selling points" that make you unique. Commit those qualities to memory and write them down, and practice working them into your answers.

TREAT IT LIKE A CONVERSATION

Many people, if not most, approach interviews like they are interrogations. This is particularly true for introverts, who are probably already more than a little tense and stressed out, which is understandable, because there is a lot at stake during a job interview (that whole "I need a paycheck so I can eat" thing). But tensing up like you're handcuffed to a table, giving short, terse answers like you're afraid of implicating yourself in a crime, and seeming to be generally terrified is not going to help you. What will help you is to approach the interview like a discussion or conversation

Small Talk

Unfortunately, a standard part of most interviews is small talk, something most introverts are not entirely fond of. If you've read through the previous chapters (and I'm assuming that you have), then you know how to handle small talk, at least in theory, as well as why it's important, so we won't go over that again. In a job interview situation, however, small talk can serve a different purpose, and it can even be a powerful and helpful tool. Think about the role that small talk usually plays: it's a conversation starter, an introductory phase that, when done correctly, can gradually lead to more in-depth discussion. In a job interview, this little warm-up can help you to feel more comfortable with the person with whom you are interviewing, enabling you to get a good read on their personality and how they communicate. But small talk can also help to change the nature of your interpersonal interaction from a rapid-fire question-and-answer session or police interrogation into something that feels a little more natural and relaxed. So remember to pack (and practice) your small talk skills)

Ask Questions

Put those listening skills to work and pay attention to everything the interviewer says. Process this information; let it inform your own opinion about the job and the company. Remember: the interview is just as much about you seeing if the company is a good fit for you as much as it is about the company seeing if you are what they need. However, don't just sit there and listen—don't forget that this is a conversation, and conversations require at least two parties. Instead, engage with the interviewer in the same way in which he/she is engaging with you by asking questions, preferably ones that are tailored to the company and the industry (that's where the information gathering and listening can really pay off). This shows that you have genuine interest in the company/job position, that you understand the industry and what the business does, and that you're taking the interview seriously and paying attention. Additionally, you can also ask about the interviewer's own personal opinions on a certain business-related topic.

If you're like me, a person whose brains seems to freeze at the worst possible times (like during job interviews), you may find it helpful to write down some questions that you think are likely to be relevant to the interview. For example, if you work in a field that uses industry-specific software, you can ask about which software that particular company uses.

LEARN HOW TO SELF-PROMOTE

Most introverts aren't wired to be naturally effective self-promoters. We're listeners who tend to only get personal with a small group of people. I, for example, am so bad at self-promotion that I have actually talked myself out of being hired. And while I'm better at it now, I still hate it and find it distasteful. But it's a necessary skill, so here are a few tips on how to sell yourself without feeling like a shady used car salesman.

It's Not Bragging If It's True

This is the first hurdle you have to get over—the concern that you're being a braggart. Speaking positively about yourself isn't bragging. You're stating facts (unless you're lying, in which case you're not bragging, you're being misleading). Bragging is when someone obnoxiously gushes about themselves, whether it's a skill they have or an item they possess, in an attempt to feel superior over others. Simply telling an interviewer what makes you qualified to fill a certain role or do a particular job, whether you're talking about your skillset or work experience, is just you answering a question.

Repeat What Others Have Said

This is a helpful tip if you have trouble thinking of your most notable and valuable skills and if you still feel uncomfortable talking about yourself. Ask yourself this question: "What have others praised me for? What positive qualities are commented on most often?" If you're one of those people who has trouble identifying their own strengths, relying on what others have told you is the best way to get an accurate idea of what the outside world sees as your stand-out qualities.

Present Evidence; Be Specific

Anyone can say that they are an "efficient worker" or that they're "good communicators", but those are just words. Not only that, they're vague phrases; "good communicator" could mean that you've mediated disputes between Israel and Palestine and brought peace to the Holy Land or it could mean that you know how to type a readable email that won't get you reported to HR. So when you're in an interview and get asked a question like, "What are your qualifications", or "What would you say are greatest strengths?" shore up standard, "I'm skilled in _____" replies with examples of how you have applied those skills in such a way as to make a positive impact on current or former places of employment. For example, let's say that you're applying to be an office assistant or manager. Telling your interviewer that you're "good with computers" is a good start, but it's also something that almost everyone says, so take it further and give examples. Explain how, at your current job, you cut down on the need to call repairmen by learning how to fix the computers, printers, and other office equipment, thus saving the company a lot of time and money. Or tell them about how you turned your current employer's website from an Angelfire-era nightmare of blinking graphics and blinding colors into a sleek, well-designed, functional, and popular page.

THE SOCIALLY COMPETENT INTROVERT

I mentioned earlier that a common misconception is that introverts are sad, lonely, and shy people who would love to be "part of the group", but just don't know how. That's why so many of our well-meaning friends and family try to push us into social situations, saying things like, "Oh, come on now. You don't need to hide in your house; everybody there likes you and wants to see you. Don't be shy; we don't bite." But what almost any introvert will tell you is that their solitude is a choice and a preference.

Let's face it—you're probably never going to be a "people person". You're not going to be the type to actively seek out parties where you can mingle and chat with hundreds of people. You will most likely always prefer solitude, small groups, and more cerebral activities. Large gatherings will wear you out and leave you feeling like you've been hit with a bomb. That's just who you are and it's fine. The point of this book was not to turn you into a extroverted social butterfly, but to help you understand your own tendencies as an introvert and how to work with them and around them in order to be able to function and perform well in social situations. Will you always succeed? No. Are you going to embarrass yourself at some point? Probably. But that's part of the learning process. It also helps to remember that the person who obsesses the most about what you do and how you screw up is you. We are a self-absorbed people—no one is probably paying that much attention to you and they definitely aren't dwelling on it after the event has occurred. Yes, there'll always be that one person who feels the need to remind everyone of that one time you got so drunk, you started talking to the dog like it was a human, but that person is a jerk, so disregard them.

By using the strategies and tips in this book, you can grow your confidence and increase your social skills. Instead of focusing on past failures, or worrying about how you might screw up in the future, direct that energy toward practicing social skills, getting to know the people around you and the environment in which you exist, and creating a style of socializing that is tailored to fit you and your needs. Good luck in your future social endeavors and thank you for reading.

Made in the USA
Lexington, KY
27 July 2016